Mazes

For Kids

Ages 4-6

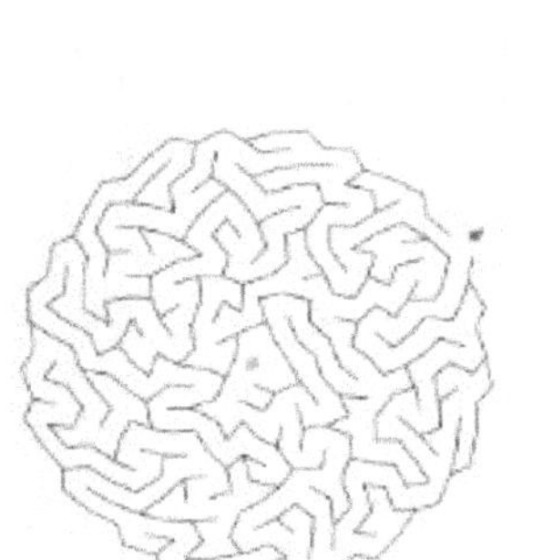

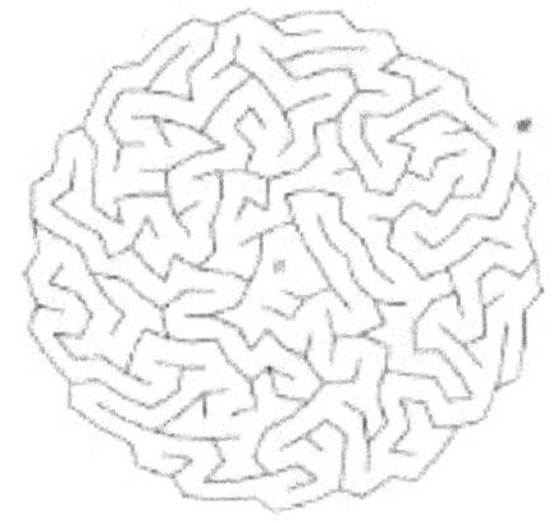

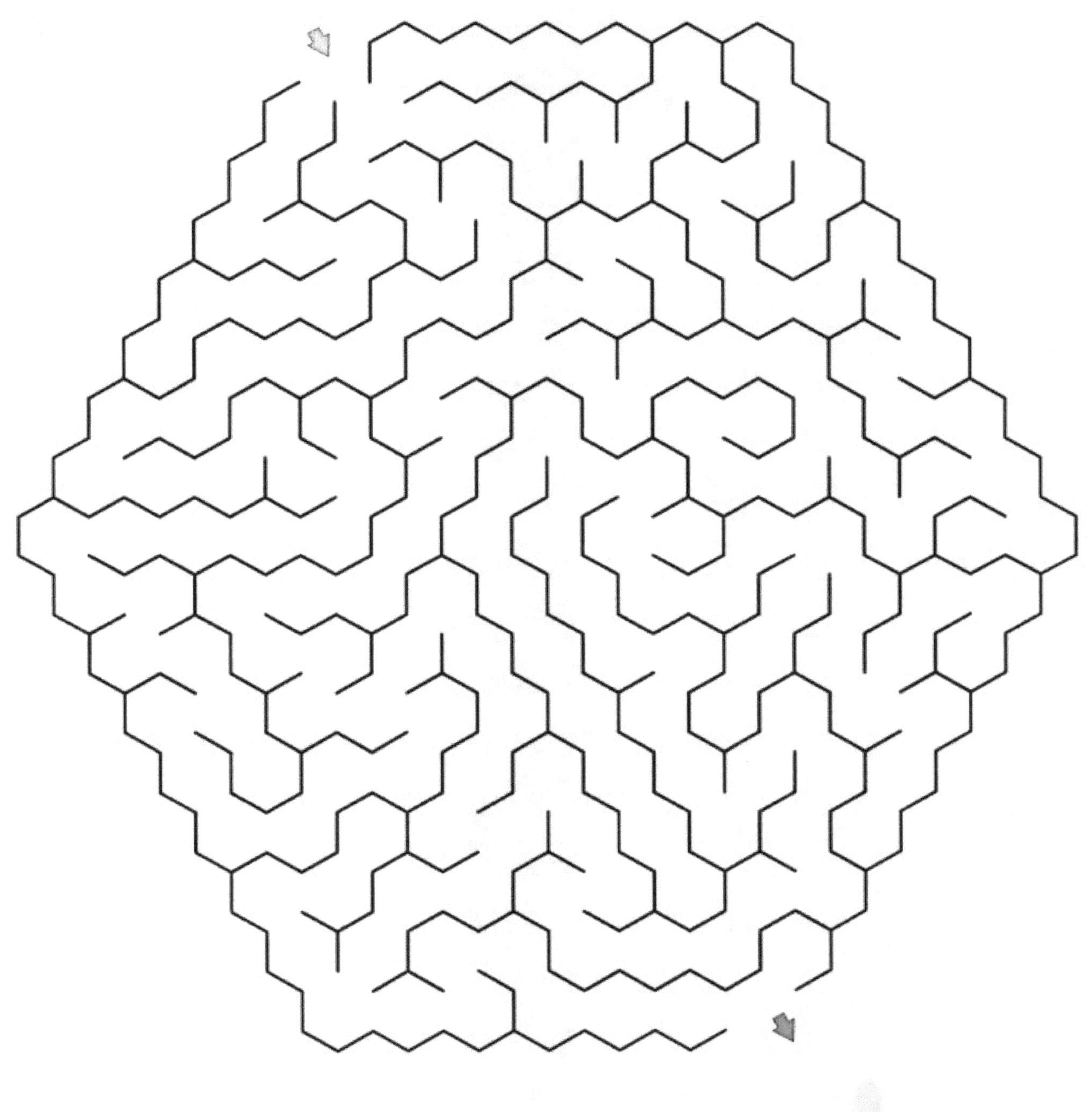

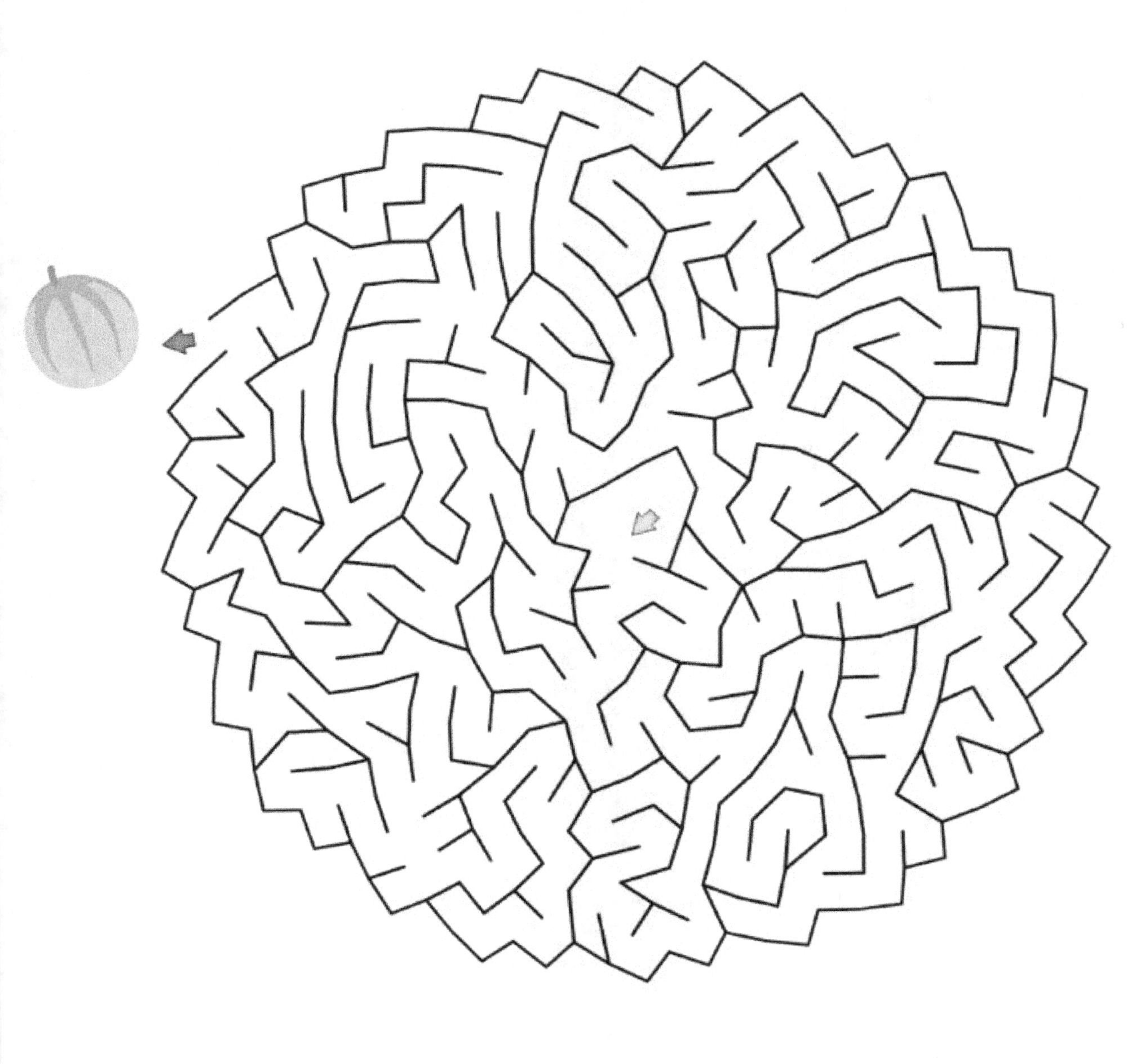

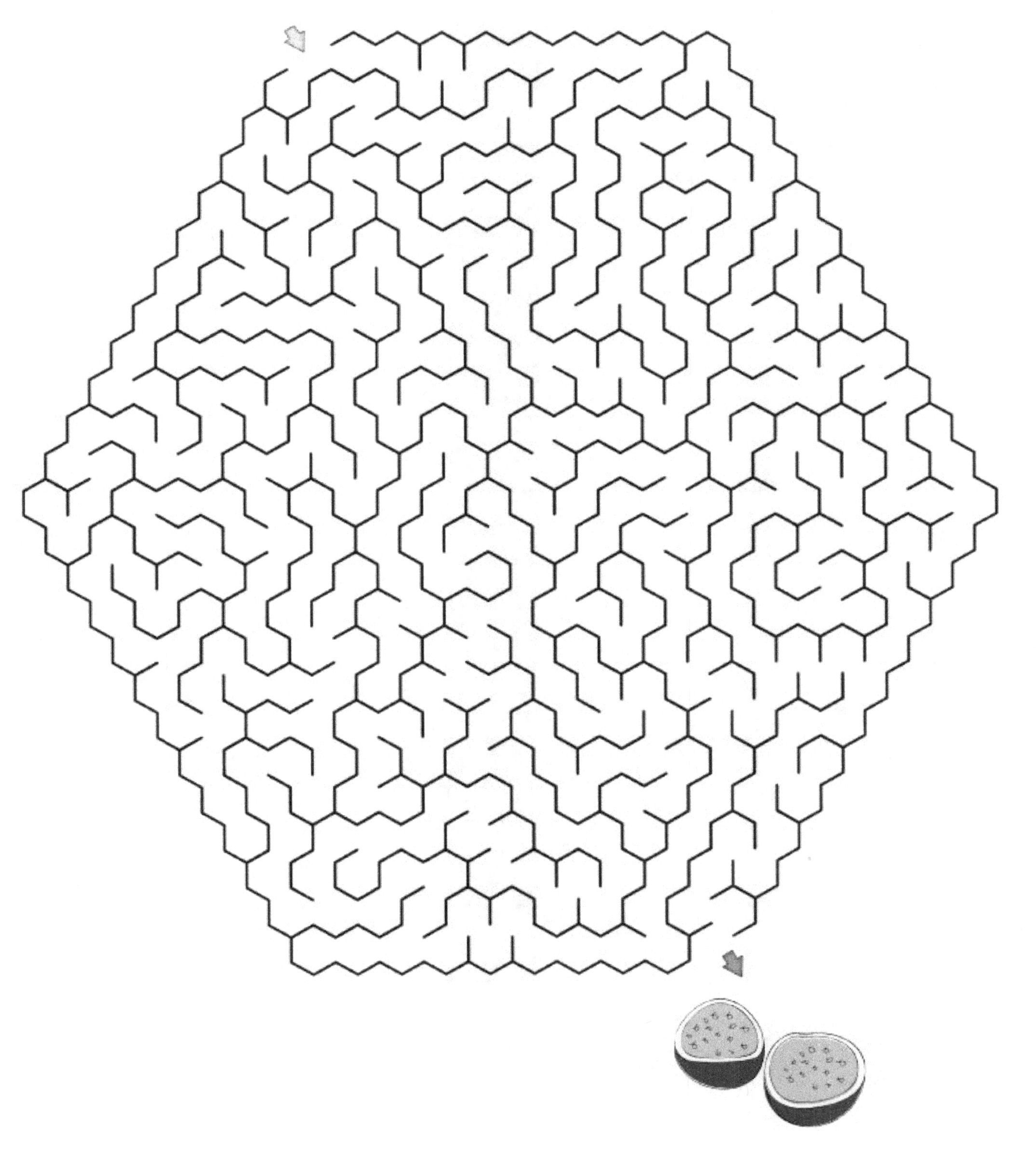

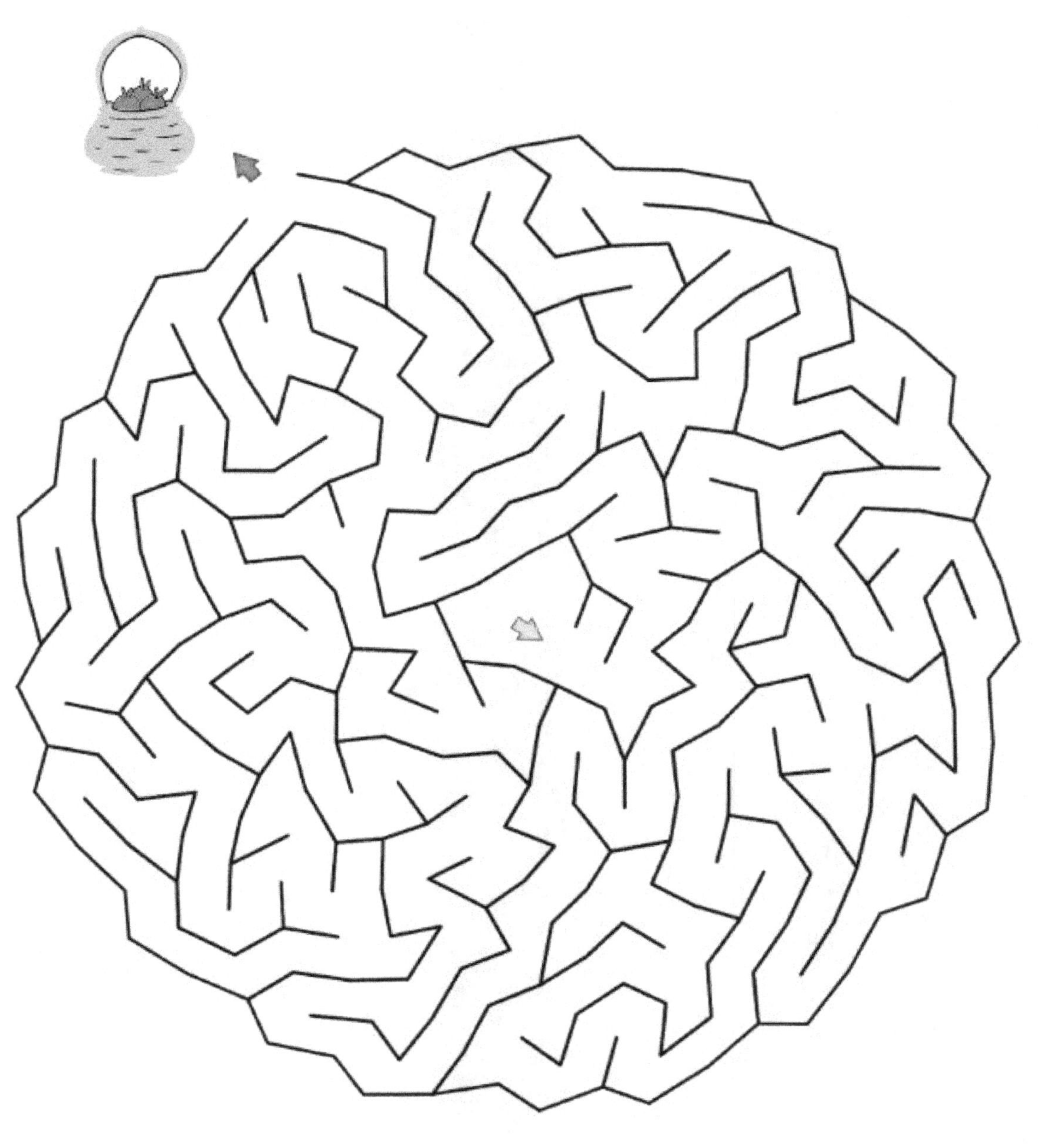

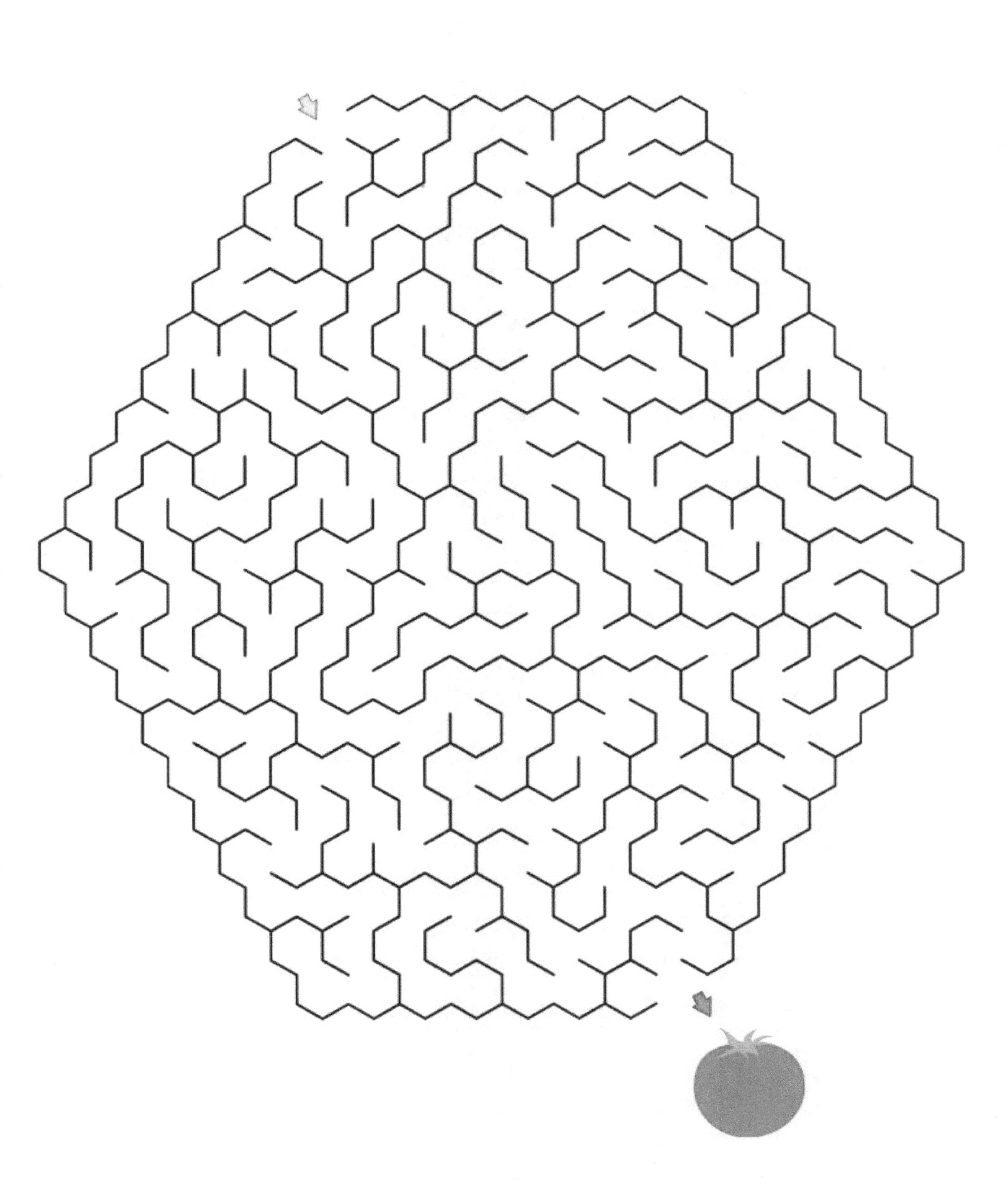

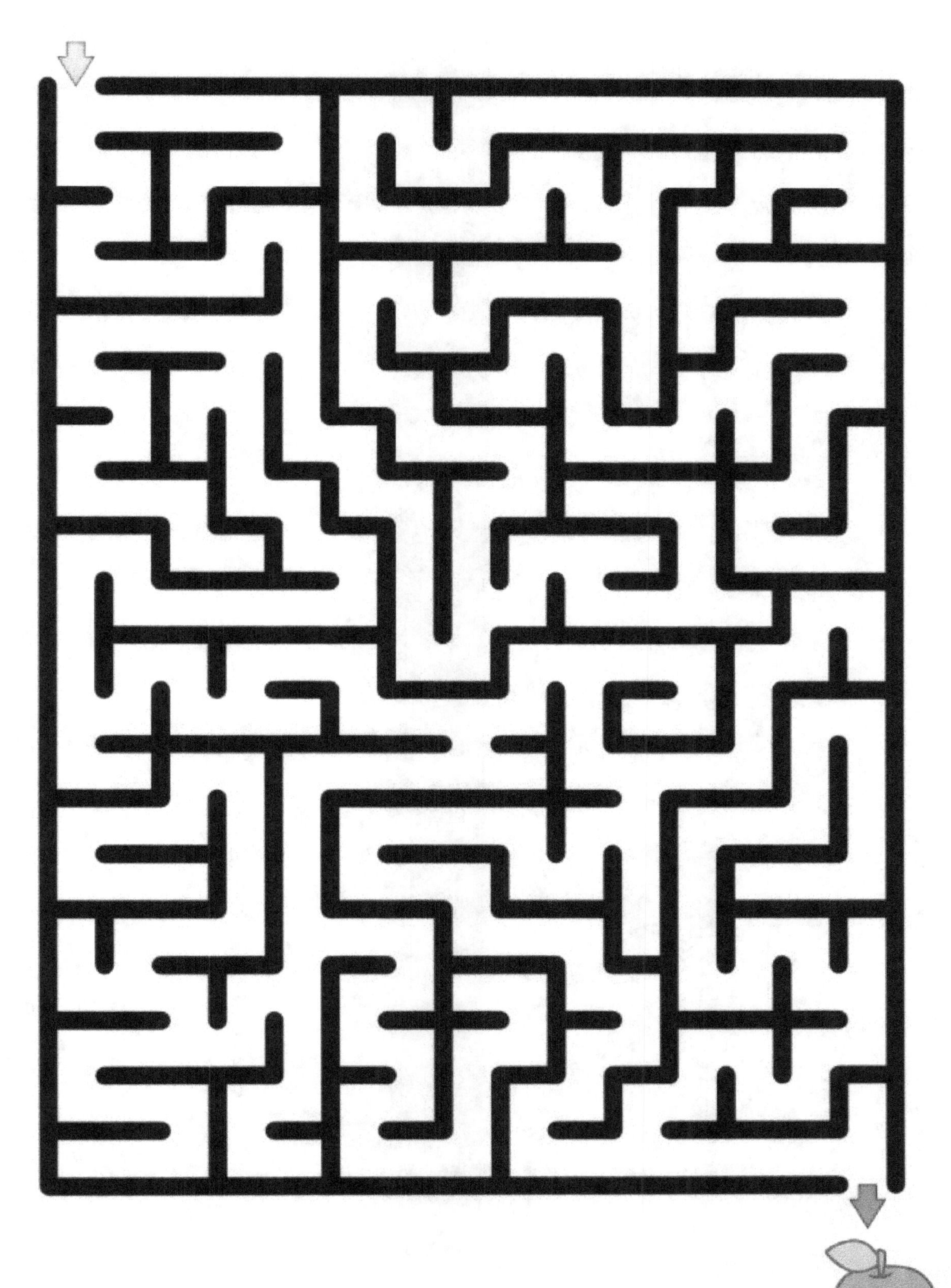

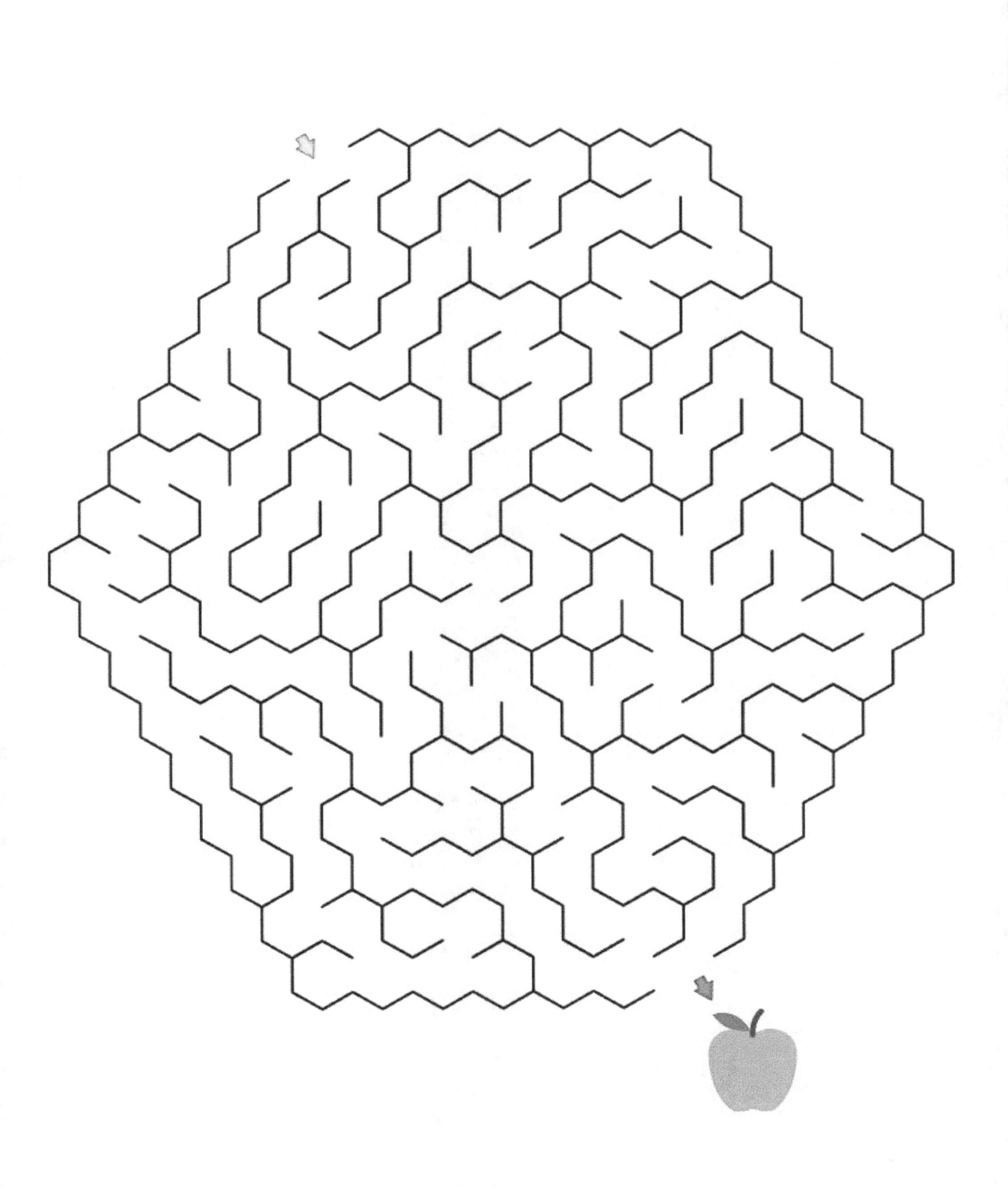

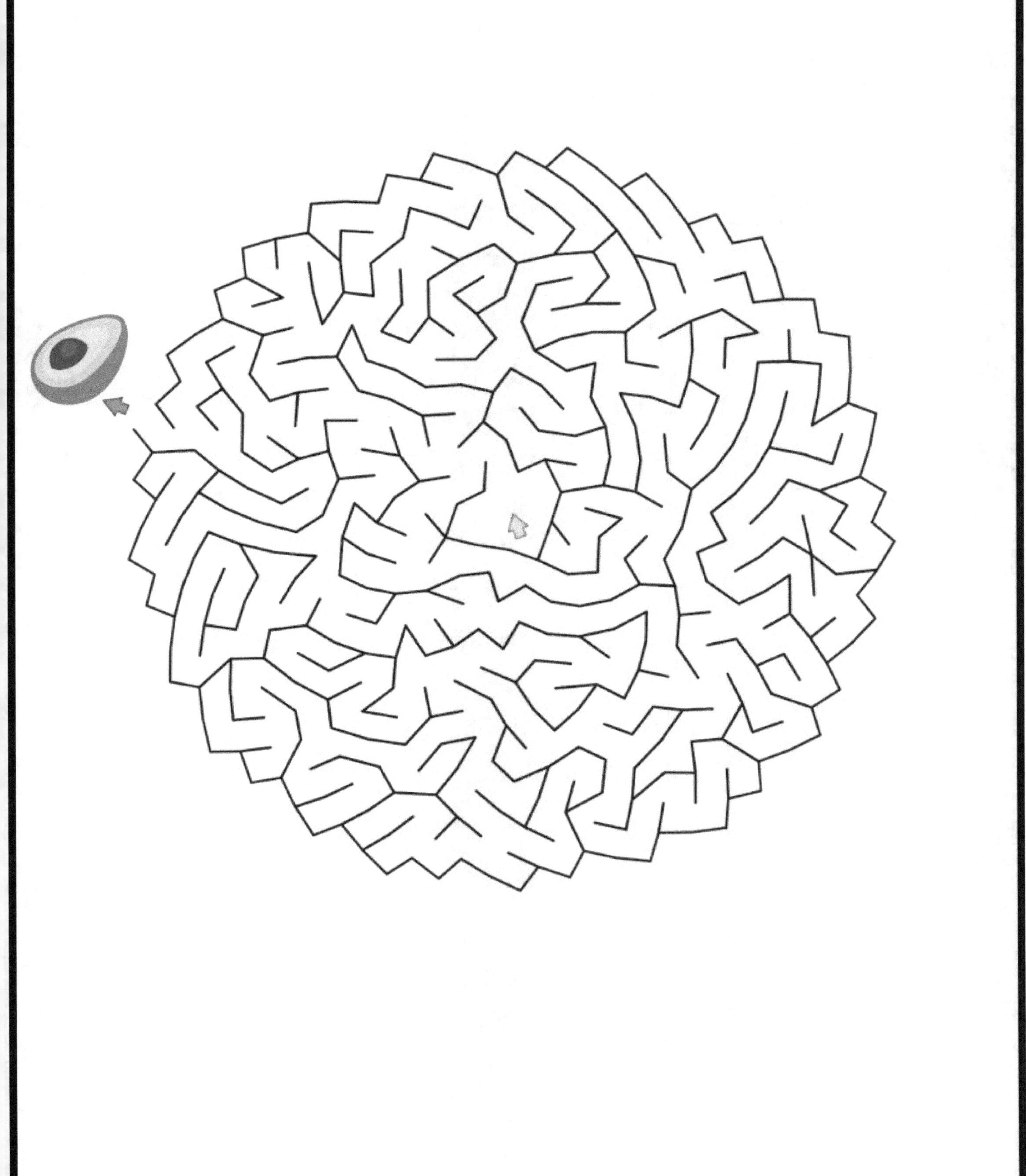